# CONTENTS

## The Official Justin Bieber Scrapbook

Welcome Beliebers! There's so much to see and do in this sensational new Scrapbook. Read up on the world's favourite pop star, then stick your photos and mementos in alongside Justin's. Check out the JB stickers at the back of the book!


THE ESSENTIAL JUSTIN 4
SUPER-FAN PROFILE 6
IT'S A FAMILY AFFAIR 8
ME AND MY WORLD 9
POP PALS 10
FRIEND FILES 14
JUSTIN AND THE MUSIC 16
LIVING LEGENDS 18
DREAM TEAM 19
THE MUSIC AND ME 20
CELEBRITY FANS 22
LOST IN LYRICS 24
NAME THAT JB TUNE! 25
KEEPING UP APPEARANCES! 26
MY TOP P.A.S 29
FASHION FORWARD 30
MY STYLE 33
JUST JUSTIN 34
SHOW-STOPPER! 36
CONCERT KEEPSAKES 40
JUSTIN' BIEBER WORD WORKOUT 42
NEVER A CROSS WORD WITH JUSTIN 43
AND THE WINNER IS... JUSTIN BIEBER! 44
NOW THE WINNER IS... ME! 47
SMALL SCREEN STAR 48
BIG SCREEN IDOL 50
TV TASTES AND FILM FAVOURITES 51
BIEBER LOVE! 52
HAPPY HOLIDAYS 54
DREAM DESTINATIONS 57
ANSWERS 58

Published By Century Books Limted,
Unit I, Upside Station Building, Solsbro Road,
Torquay, Devon. TQ2 6FD.
books@centurybooksltd.co.uk
Published 2012



www.justinbiebermusic.com
www.justinbieberstore.com
www.justinbiebermusic.com/justforyou

£4.99

# THE ESSENTIAL JUSTIN

Do you heart Bieber? To be a fully-fledged Belieber you need to know the key Justin facts. We've collected all of his deets in one handy profile…

Justin Bieber

| | |
|---|---|
| **Full name:** | Justin Drew Bieber |
| **Date of birth:** | 1st March 1994 |
| **Star sign:** | Pisces |
| **Eye colour:** | Brown |
| **Hair colour:** | Brown |
| **Twitter profile:** | @justinbieber |
| **Official website:** | www.justinbiebermusic.com |
| **Place of birth:** | London, Ontario, Canada |
| **Lives:** | Atlanta, Georgia, USA |
| **Family:** | Mum Pattie Mallette |
| | Dad Jeremy Bieber |
| | Sister Jazmyn |
| | Brother Jaxon |
| **Favourite sport:** | Basketball |
| **Hidden talent:** | Justin claims he can solve a Rubik's Cube in under a minute |
| **Favourite TV show:** | *Smallville* |
| **Favourite food:** | Spaghetti |
| **Instruments played:** | Guitar, piano, drums and trumpet |

# SUPER-FAN PROFILE

Now we know all of Justin's vital statistics, let's find out about you! Fill this page with info, photos and doodles about you and your world.

Full name:

Date of birth:

Star sign:

Eye colour:

Hair colour:

Place of birth:

Lives:

Family:

Pets:

Favourite sport:

Hidden talent:

Favourite TV show:

Favourite food:

Instruments played:

## Justin And Me:

I think JB is the greatest because

# IT'S A FAMILY AFFAIR

Family means everything to Justin. Let's meet his nearest and dearest...

## Mummy's Boy!

These days, JB's devoted mum Pattie Mallette is a constant touring companion. She makes sure that he doesn't get into too much trouble on the road!

## Dad's A Legend!

Justin also spends lots of time with his dad Jeremy Bieber and his baby brother and sister. Even though his parents split up when he was young, they are all still very close.

## All Together Now

Justin has a big extended family, too. Whenever he has a break in his schedule, Justin loves to hang out in Stratford with his grandparents, Diane and Bruce Dale.

Who are the peoplc that have always been there for you?
Stick in or draw pictures about your fabulous fam!

# POP PALS

Since exploding on the scene in 2010, Justin Bieber has got to hang out and make friends with some of the most famous faces in the world. Get ready to meet a few of Justin's sparkling BFFs...

# JUSTIN BIEBER

## USHER

The first celebrity Belieber was undoubtedly R&B star Usher Raymond. Usher was passed a tape of an early Justin song and quickly recognised the youngster's potential, immediately signing him to his record label. He has been a constant friend and mentor ever since. Justin admits he often turns to Usher for advice, encouragement and a few wise words.

## BUSTA RHYMES!

Justin has collaborated with a wide range of musicians during his career, but he has especially fond memories of his work with New York rapper Busta Rhymes. The pair struck up a friendship when they recorded 'Drummer Boy' for Justin's album, 'Under The Mistletoe'. Recently, Justin has been showing off some impressive rapping skills – perhaps his friend has been giving him lessons?

## SEAN KINGSTON

Justin is often snapped having fun with his good friend Sean Kingston. The pair recorded together on Justin's first album and have stayed pals ever since. When they meet up at award shows, they get to be fans themselves, grabbing pictures with passing celebs. Here they are posing with supermodel Tyra Banks.

## TAYLOR SWIFT!

Justin is great friends with American singer-songwriter Taylor Swift. The pair have toured together and often joined each other on stage for duets. They also can't resist hooking up to share a chat and a joke – check out their YouTube videos for proof!

## JADEN SMITH

Another of Justin's good friends is Jaden Smith, movie star Will Smith's oldest son. The pair worked together on Never Say Never and even recorded a special 'Happy New Year' track together last year. Here are the pals hanging out with LMFAO's Redfoo at the 2011 American Music Awards.

POP PALS
Justin Bieber

# JUSTIN BIEBER

KATY PERRY

Katy and Justin hit it off after meeting on the road, carrying on their friendship over Twitter. Katy made the news when she admitted she liked Justin so much she wanted to adopt him!

TAIO CRUZ

UK star Taio was one of a number of people who were asked to write music for Justin's new album 'Believe'. The pair got to spend some time together in Los Angeles, along with Sean Kingston. Afterwards Taio promised to write a track that was 'young and fun' – just like Justin himself!

PITBULL

Justin is huge fan of hip hop music and has got to know a heap of rap stars. Here's a picture of JB hanging out with Miami artist Pitbull at a New Year's Eve party.

WILL FERREL

Thanks to the box office hit Justin Bieber – Never Say Never 3D he's made friends with some movie stars too! Justin met Will Ferrell when the funnyman pranked him at the US Open Tennis Championships. Since then the boys have tried to play jokes on each other whenever their paths have crossed.

WILL.I.AM

JB got the chance to spend time with a stellar line up of celebrities when he took part in recording 'We Are The World 25 For Haiti' - a charity song to raise funds for the Haiti earthquake appeal. Since then Black Eyed Peas star will.i.am and Justin have started working together.

Who's who in your crew? Everybody needs good friends! Make these pages a special place crammed with facts and stats about all of your favourite people. Draw or stick a photo at the top of each file, then fill in all the essential details

**Name:** ..........

**Birthday:** ..........

**How we met:** ..........

..........

..........

**Their best quality** ..........

..........

**Funny fact:** ..........

..........

..........

**Good times we've shared:** ..........

..........

..........

..........

..........

**Why they'll always be my friend:** ..........

..........

..........

..........

..........

..........

**Name:** ..........

**Birthday:** ..........

**How we met:** ..........

..........

..........

**Their best quality** ..........

..........

**Funny fact:** ..........

..........

..........

**Good times we've shared:** ..........

..........

..........

..........

..........

**Why they'll always be my friend:** ..........

..........

..........

..........

..........

..........

Name:

Birthday:

How we met:

Their best quality

Funny fact:

Good times we've shared:

Why they'll always be my friend:

Name:

Birthday:

How we met:

Their best quality

Funny fact:

Good times we've shared:

Why they'll always be my friend:

# JUSTIN AND THE MUSIC

Despite all his fame and fortune, Justin is at his happiest when he's making music. Luckily for us, singing, writing songs and playing instruments has been a life-long passion for JBiebz! With with his third full album soon to be released, that passion looks set to continue way into the future!

Must record vocals to...

my dream duets!

## The Musician

Justin prides himself on being able to play a whole variety of instruments. While he freely admits that he only dabbles on some, he often talks about his love of finding new ways to make up melodies and compose songs.

## The Leftie

Being left-handed can make playing the guitar a little trickier than it is for right-handers. When Justin strums his acoustic, the strings have to be arranged the other way up to standard models - not that this stops JB from making an awesome sound!

## The Composer

During his rare hours of downtime, Justin can usually be found sitting in front of a piano. The pop prince can't resist picking out new tunes on the keyboard or working out new arrangements.

## The Singer

Despite all his instrumental skills, Justin is a vocalist first and foremost. He started singing at the age of six! By twelve, JB was recording songs and uploading them to YouTube. His route to stardom was sealed when music exec Scooter Braun saw one of these vids and asked to meet him!

What are your musical talents? Write about them here...

# JUSTIN BIEBER

# LIVING LEGENDS

**Now Justin is a global star, he gets invited to work with some of the finest producers and musicians out there. Here are just four of the legends that he's been collaborating with recently.**

Timbaland = @Timbaland

Timbaland has produced hit records for scores of artists as well as topping the charts himself. This guy has laid down tunes for Nelly Furtado, Justin Timberlake, Madonna and Missy Elliot! Timbaland hit it off with JB straight away, impressed by the young star's dedication to making music.

Drake = @Drake

You probably recognise rapper Drake from his guest spots on tracks with the likes of Rihanna and Eminem. There's no word yet on what he's been cooking up with Justin, but it's sure to be something tasty!

Lil Wayne = @LilTunechi

As well as being one of the world's most successful rappers, Lil Wayne has also guested on lots of other artist's tunes. Justin revealed he was working with Lil Wayne when he tweeted a picture of them hanging out outside the studio with their skateboards!

Kanye West = @kanyewest

Kanye and Justin have already worked together on a remix of the song 'Runaway'. Word has now leaked that the pair will also reunite for Justin's new album 'Believe'.

For a closer glimpse into JB's world, check out each of these artists' Twitter accounts too - they often chat with @justinbieber about their latest sessions!

# ☆DREAM TEAM☆

Aside from bags of talent, one of the keys to Justin's incredible rise to fame has been his tightknit crew. Manager Scooter and mentor Usher, along with JB's mum Pattie, have helped turn a passionate young musician into a glittering A-list superstar! Justin knows that wherever his career takes him, his team will be there to offer advice and support every step of the way.

## MY DREAM TEAM

Who are on hand to help you be the best you can be? Write down the names of three people that have helped you develop your skills and talents.

1.

2.

3.

# THE MUSIC AND ME

Justin's tunes can make us rock to the beat, cheer us up when we're down or even get us thinking about someone special. Being a Belieber is totally infectious! What does JB's music mean to you?

My favourite Justin Bieber song is

..................................................................

My favourite JB lyric is

..................................................................

When I'm feeling blue the song that always makes me smile is

..................................................................

The tune I play when I want to chill is

..................................................................

The best number to dance like crazy to is

..................................................................

The Justin song my friends and I sing together has got to be

..................................................................

## Justin Bieber 4Ever!

JB is the best because

Do you have a song hiding inside of you? Let JB inspire you to get creative! Use this page to compose the lyrics for a brand new number, written by you.

Song Title:

Written by:

Style of music:

# CELEBRITY FANS

As well as having a host of celebrity friends, Biebz has a legion of A-list fans, too!

Barack Obama

With two teenage daughters it's no surprise that the American President knows all about Justin Bieber! He showed he was a fan too when he asked JB to attend an ultra-V.I.P. Christmas party in Washington in 2011.

Kim Kardashian

Reality TV star Kim Kardashian shocked the world when she admitted she was suffering from Bieber fever! She posted so many messages about JB on her Twitter that people even thought the pair were an item!

Jennifer Hudson

Since meeting Justin, American Idol star Jennifer has told anyone that will listen what a huge fan she is. I do have Bieber fever. He is the most adorable, sweetest, oh he's so sweet

Goofy

Justin was mobbed by Disney characters when he took part in a Christmas Day Parade TV Special - can't get more famous than that!

Like Justin, Shania Twain hails from a small town in Ontario, Canada. She is such an avid supporter of JB's career, she even asked to present a trophy with him at the CMT Awards in 2011.

People were worried rapper and actor Common had it in for Justin when they met at a celebrity basketball match. Justin fell over during the game and people suspected Common was to blame. However, Bieber was quick to explain that he had simply tripped! Common later went on record to say he was a Belieber!

Pirates Of The Caribbean star Johnny Depp was spotted in the audience during Justin's show at Miami's American Airlines Arena in 2010. Johnny tried to keep a low profile, but Justin spotted the movie star and dedicated his performance of 'Baby' to him!

Are there any more superstar Beliebers out there? Write down the names of the celebs you'd love to spot singing along in the crowd at Justin's next gig!

..............................................................

..............................................................

..............................................................

..............................................................

..............................................................

..............................................................

..............................................................

# JUSTIN BIEBER

# LOST IN LYRICS

Everyone can hum along to Justin's jams, but how well do you really know the Bieber back catalogue? Find a pen, then fill in the gaps in these classic tunes.

1. Are we an item? Girl, quit playin:
_ _'_ _ _ _ _ _ _ _ _ _ _ _ _ _; what are you sayin'?

2. Your lips, _ _ _ _ _ _ _ _ _ _ _ _ _ _ _ _ _
Shouldn't have let you know.

3. Whenever you knock me down
I will not _ _ _ _ _ _ _ _ _ _ _ _ _ _ _.

4. Yeah I'm on the drum yeah I'm on the snare drum,
Yeah _'_ _ _ _ _ _ _ _ _ _ _ cause the beat goes dumb.

5. When I met you girl, I tried to pay for dinner,
Pulled out your card, I thought _ _ _ _ _ _ _ _ _ _ _.

6. Do you not think so far ahead?
'Cause I been thinkin' about _ _ _ _ _ _ _.

7. I never understood you when you'd say,
You wanted me to _ _ _ _ _ _ _ _ _ _ _ _ _ _.

8. My prize possession, one and only,
_ _ _ _ _ _ _ _ _ _ _ _, I want you.

9. And so, I'm offering this simple phrase,
To kids from _ _ _ _ _ _ _ _ _ _ _-_ _ _

10. See my baby really needs some help,
'Cause she can never _ _ _ _ _ _ _ _ _ _ _ _ _ _ _

# NAME THAT JB TUNE!

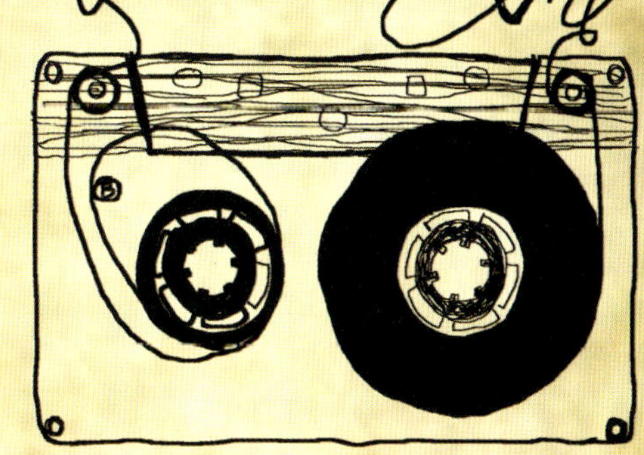


Justin's albums are filled with an addictive list of tracks! Draw a line to match each set of lyrics with the JB tune it comes from. Which ones have you got on your playlist right now?

|  |  |
|---|---|
| 1. She's indecisive, she can't decide, She keeps on looking from left to right. | A. All I Want For Christmas Is You |
| 2. All the lights are shining so brightly everywhere, And the sound of children's laughter fills the air. | B. Baby |
| 3. I don't wanna miss out on the holiday, But I can't stop staring at your face. | C. Pray |
| 4. Yeah, I got a PHD I don't need a fake ID, Yeah you females know of me I'm so sick with no IV. | D. Mistletoe |
| 5. I'm just trying to be cool, cool, cool, Trying to be cool, whatcha expect me to do? | E. Never Say Never |
| 6. And I wanna play it cool, but I'm losin' you, I'll buy you anything, I'll buy you any ring. | F. Runaway Love |
| 7. 'Cause I know there's sunshine behind that rain, I know there's good times behind that pain. | G. Eenie Meenie |
| 8. I'm strong enough to climb the highest tower, And I'm fast enough to run across the sea. | H. Dr Bieber |

# KEEPING UP APPEARANCES!

As an international star, Justin gets invited to the best parties, prèmieres and award ceremonies! The pop star has already met some incredible people and been to some truly amazing places. Where will he appear next?

### CHRISTMAS IN WASHINGTON 2011 WITH THE OBAMAS AND CEE LO

Not many people get invited to sing Christmas carols with the President of the United States and his family! JB ranks his time at the White House among his proudest moments ever.

### TURNING ON WESTFIELD'S CHRISTMAS LIGHTS

Justin was the first celebrity to be asked to switch on the Christmas lights at the newly-built Westfield Stratford shopping centre in London in 2011. Thousands of fans made the trip to watch the big moment! Justin made it a night they'd all remember by treating the crowds to an exclusive acoustic performance of his biggest hits.

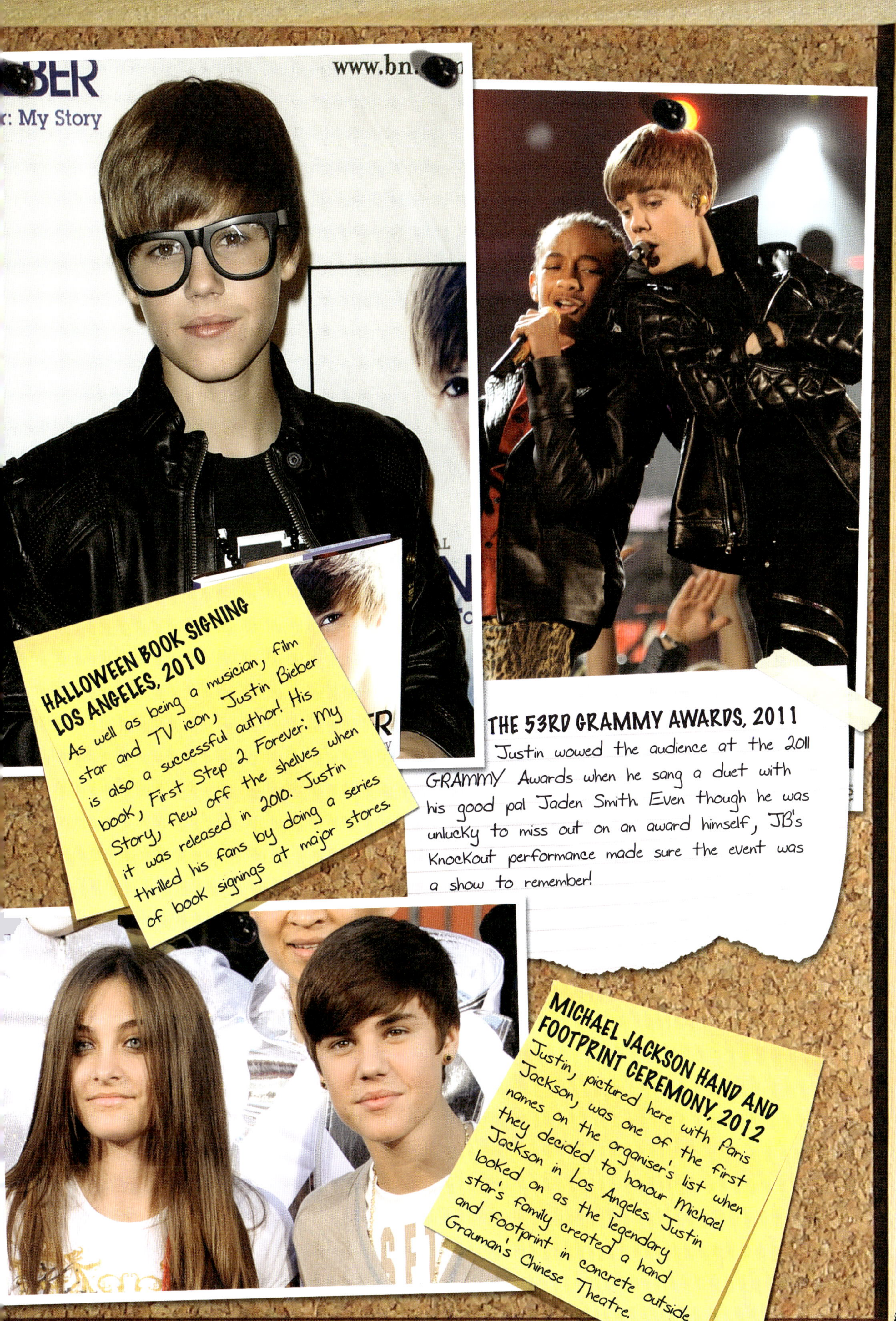


**HALLOWEEN BOOK SIGNING LOS ANGELES, 2010**

As well as being a musician, film star and TV icon, Justin Bieber is also a successful author! His book, First Step 2 Forever: My Story, flew off the shelves when it was released in 2010. Justin thrilled his fans by doing a series of book signings at major stores.

**THE 53RD GRAMMY AWARDS, 2011**

Justin wowed the audience at the 2011 GRAMMY Awards when he sang a duet with his good pal Jaden Smith. Even though he was unlucky to miss out on an award himself, JB's KnocKout performance made sure the event was a show to remember!

**MICHAEL JACKSON HAND AND FOOTPRINT CEREMONY, 2012**

Justin, pictured here with Paris Jackson, was one of the first names on the organiser's list when they decided to honour Michael Jackson in Los Angeles. Justin looked on as the legendary star's family created a hand and footprint in concrete outside Grauman's Chinese Theatre.

## THE US X FACTOR LIVE FINALE, 2011

When the US version of the X Factor needed to add some sparkle to their live finale, Justin was the obvious choice. JB was happy to oblige, especially when he got the chance to perform with contestant Drew Ryniewicz and his own singing hero, Stevie Wonder.

## MADAME TUSSAUD'S, 2011

Fancy laying a kiss on Justin? Well, if ever you're in New York, you can... sort of! A full-size waxwork of Justin Bieber has been the star attraction of Madame Tussaud's since it was unveiled by the man himself in early 2011.

# MY TOP P.A.s'

IT'S TIME TO REMEMBER SOME OF YOUR GREATEST PERSONAL APPEARANCES! HAVE YOU EVER PERFORMED ON STAGE, TAKEN PART IN A SPORTS MATCH OR VISITED SOMEWHERE EXTRA-SPECIAL? USE THIS PAGE TO WRITE ALL ABOUT YOUR FAVOURITE DAYS. FILL IN THE BOXES, DRAW PICTURES AND STICK IN PHOTOS OR NEWSPAPER CLIPPINGS.

WHERE: ..............................

WHEN: ..............................

WHY WAS IT SPECIAL? ..............................

..............................

..............................

..............................

WHO WAS THERE? ..............................

..............................

THE MEMORY I'LL TREASURE FOREVER

..............................

..............................

WHERE: ..............................

WHEN: ..............................

WHY WAS IT SPECIAL? ..............................

..............................

..............................

..............................

WHO WAS THERE? ..............................

..............................

..............................

THE MEMORY I'LL TREASURE FOREVER

..............................

..............................

..............................

WHERE: ..............................

WHEN: ..............................

WHY WAS IT SPECIAL? ..............................

..............................

..............................

..............................

WHO WAS THERE? ..............................

..............................

THE MEMORY I'LL TREASURE FOREVER

..............................

..............................

WHERE: ..............................

WHEN: ..............................

WHY WAS IT SPECIAL? ..............................

..............................

..............................

..............................

WHO WAS THERE? ..............................

..............................

THE MEMORY I'LL TREASURE FOREVER

..............................

..............................

# FASHION FORWARD

Justin really is the full package! Not only is he famous around the world for his music, the Bieber sense of style makes headlines, too.

## Smart And Sassy

You can't be scruffy when you're singing for the President! Justin plumped for a classic white tuxedo jacket and black trousers for his visit to the White House. Instead of the traditional bow tie, Justin brought the look up-to-date with a loosely tied straight tie.

## Hot Leather

Justin picked this Michael Jackson inspired look when he was on tour in Brazil. The slick red and black leather outfit makes him hard to miss! To complete this edgy image he added a pairof white Wayfarer sunglasses.

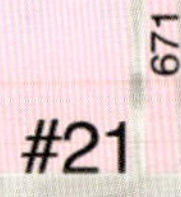

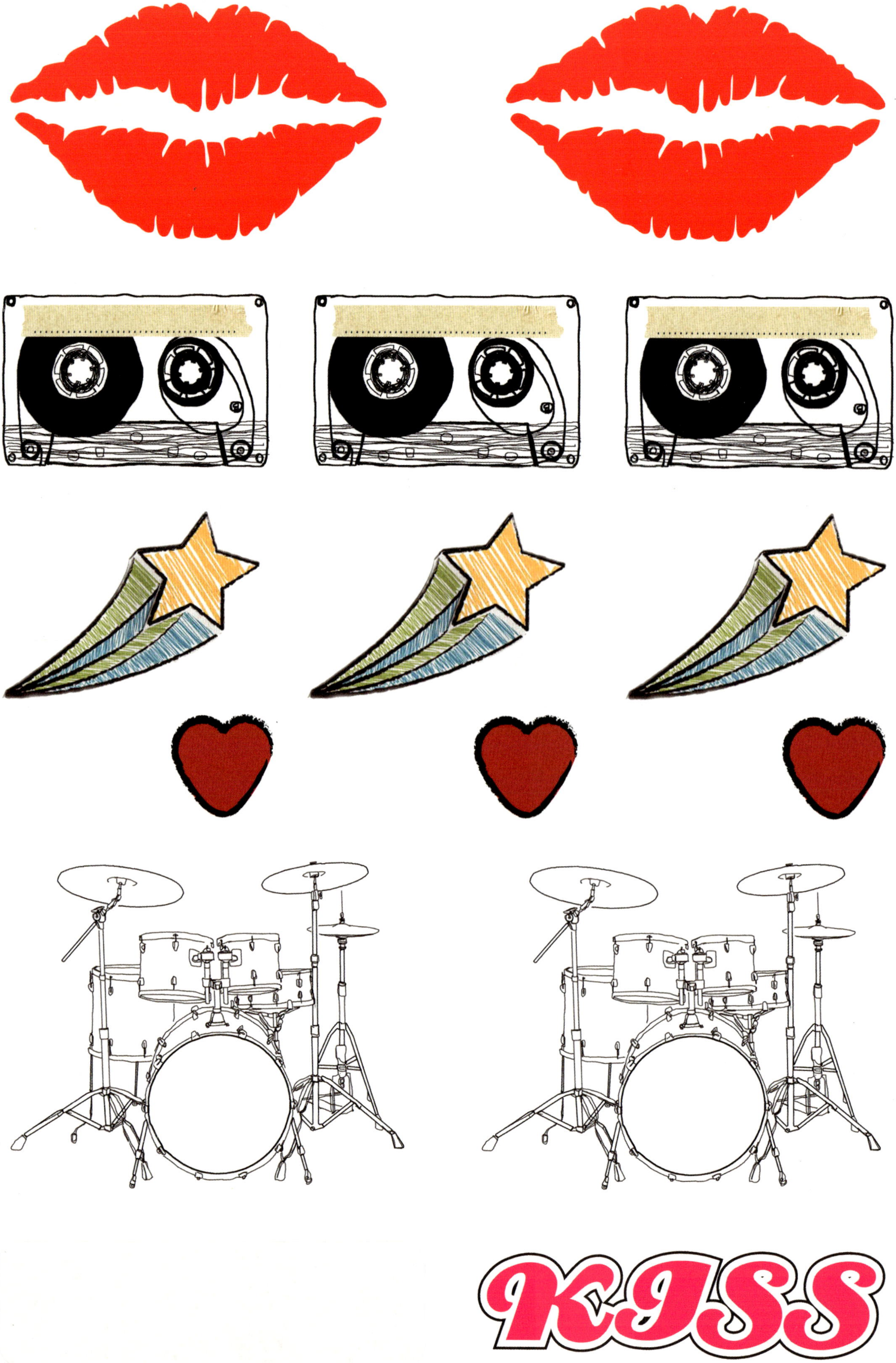

KISS

TOP SECRET

CONFIDENTIAL

CONFIDENTIAL

TOP SECRET

CONFIDENTIAL

CONFIDENTIAL

KISS

KISS

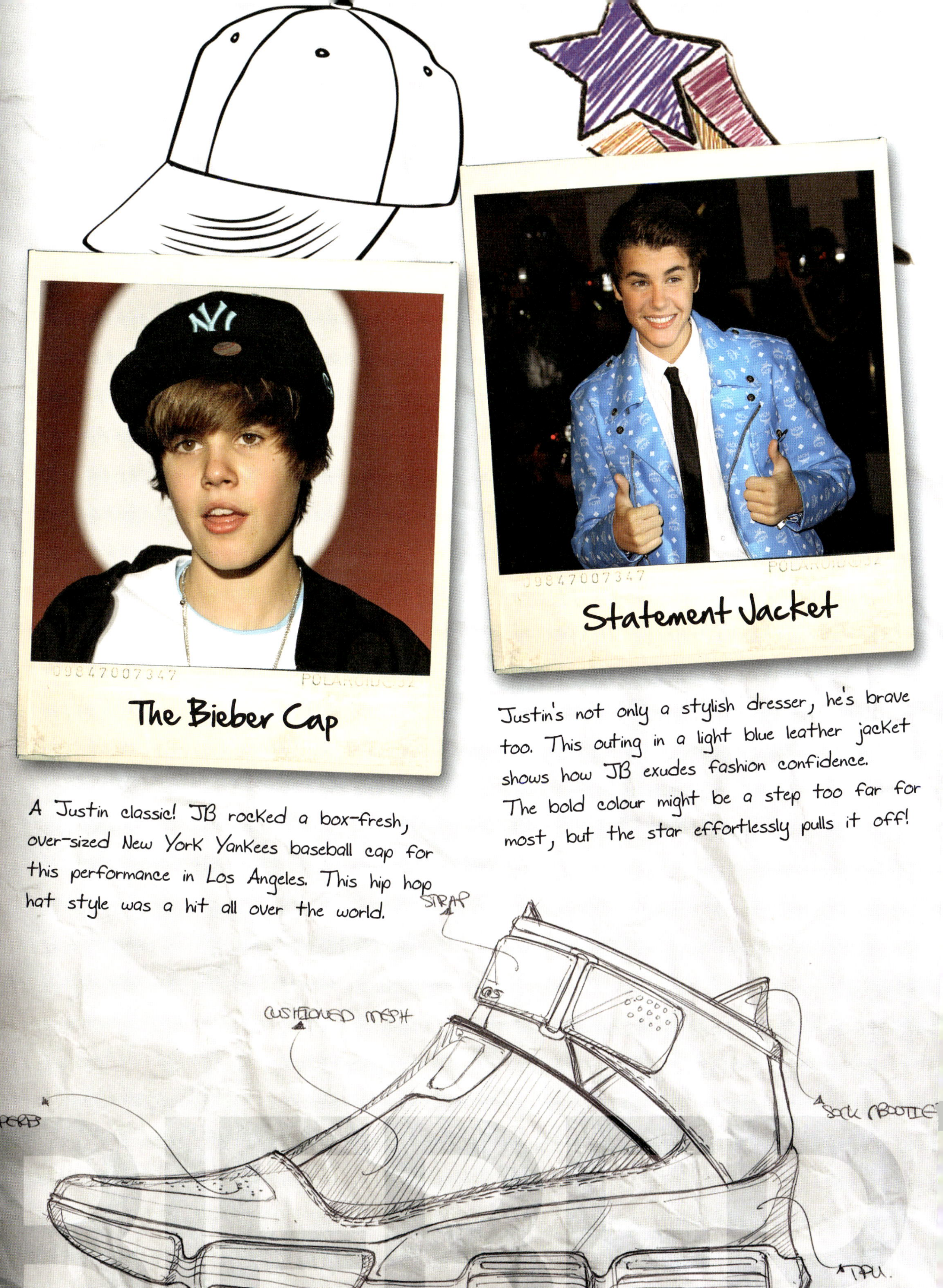


## The Bieber Cap

A Justin classic! JB rocked a box-fresh, over-sized New York Yankees baseball cap for this performance in Los Angeles. This hip hop hat style was a hit all over the world.

## Statement Jacket

Justin's not only a stylish dresser, he's brave too. This outing in a light blue leather jacket shows how JB exudes fashion confidence. The bold colour might be a step too far for most, but the star effortlessly pulls it off!

# JUSTIN BIEBER

Future Cool

On paper lurid green, zips, black leather and fingerless gloves sounds like a terrible combination. On JB it works! Justin shows once again that you can pull off any look as long as you have the confidence.

Seal Of Approval

Arguably the most powerful person in the fashion world is Anna Wintour, the editor of Vogue magazine. So fearsome is her reputation, celebrities have been known to quake in their boots when she is near! Justin and his mum Pattie weren't phased at all however, each one happy and confident in their own style.

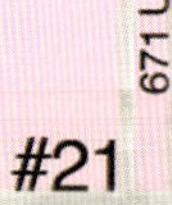

# MY STYLE

It's time to define and refine your style! Stick in some pictures of yourself, then draw arrows to the pieces you like and the bits you'd like to update. Cut pictures out of magazines for inspiration then make a shopping wish list for your next clothes trip. Don't forget to add accessories too!

JUST JUSTIN

Justin Bieber

# SHOW-STOPPER

Music has taken Justin Bieber around the world and back again. JB is a total showman who loves to engage with his fans! He practices tirelessly to make sure that every date is as fresh as his first ever gig – whether it's a stadium event or an intimate acoustic set.

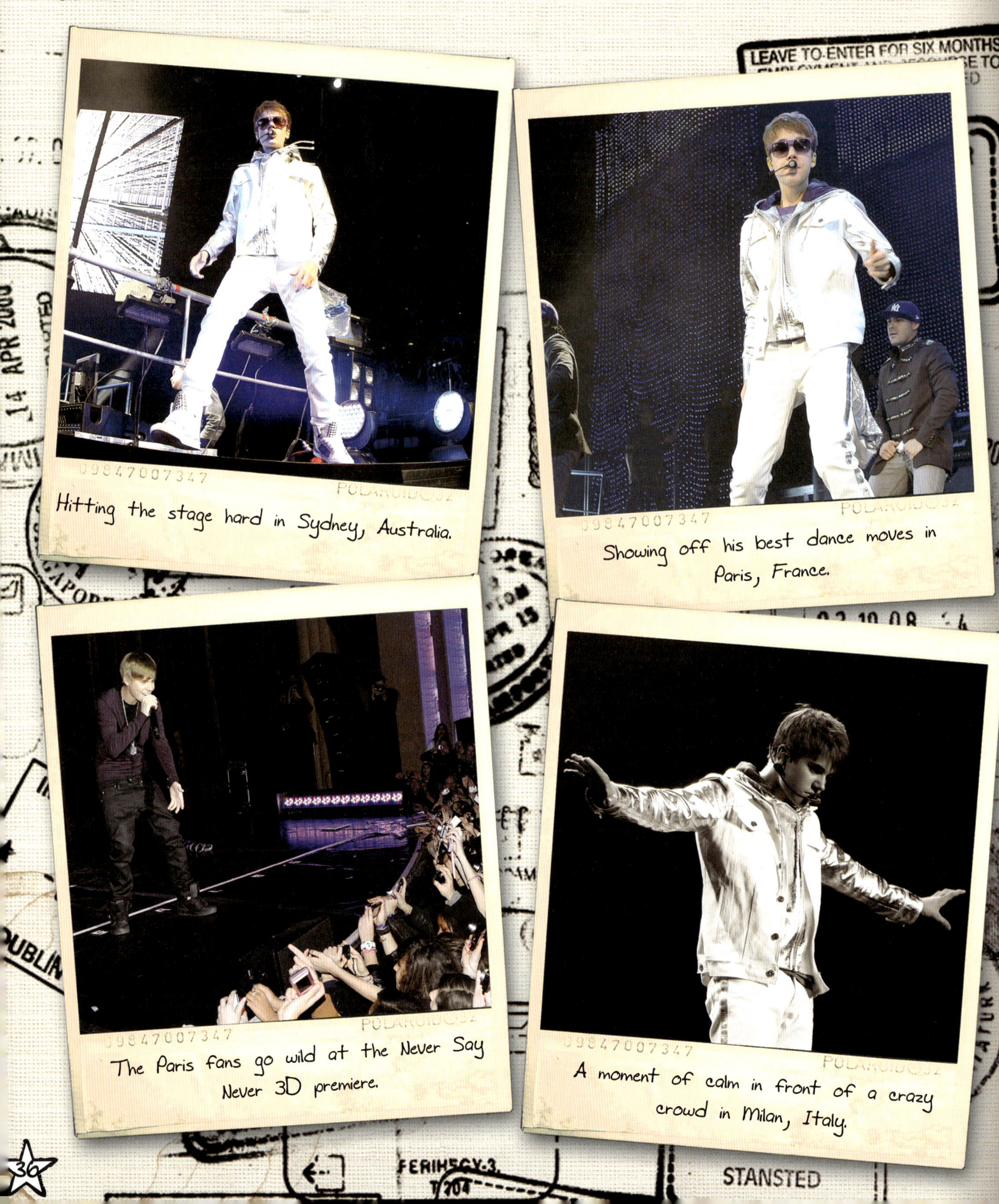


Hitting the stage hard in Sydney, Australia.

Showing off his best dance moves in Paris, France.

The Paris fans go wild at the Never Say Never 3D premiere.

A moment of calm in front of a crazy crowd in Milan, Italy.

Justin loved performing at the Bambi Awards in Berlin, Germany.

Who has Bieber fever? The London crowd, that's who!

Performing with LMFAO in Los Angeles, USA – a real highlight for Justin.

Nothing topped bringing JB's little sister Jazmyn on stage for a song in Toronto, Canada.

Giving everything on stage in Tampa, Florida.

Treating Tokyo fans to a stripped down performance.

One of many proposals Justin received during the 'My World' tour in Australia.

Justin gets up close and personal with a US crowd during an open-air performance.

JB is a massive sports fan, so being asked to perform at the 2010 Super Bowl was a huge honour.

Justin broke his foot on stage in London, but that didn't stop him rocking out in Las Vegas just days later!

Backed by a huge choir, Justin sings for President Barack Obama in Washington, USA.

A lucky Canadian gets a night to remember in Toronto.

Justin had a blast playing with legendary guitarist Carlos Santana in Times Square, New York City.

Very Important People? It doesn't get more V.I.P. than Bono, the Edge, will.i.am and Justin Bieber!

Who else's show features an exciting wire-fighting sequence?

# CONCERT KEEPSAKES

Have you been lucky enough to experience Justin Bieber live? Use these pages to record your treasured souvenirs and memories or write down what you think it might be like to go to one of his shows.

**Justin Live!**

Who I went with..........................................................

Highlight..........................................................

Mark out of ten..........................................................

My review

..........................................................

..........................................................

..........................................................

..........................................................

..........................................................

..........................................................

..........................................................

The best bits

..........................................................

..........................................................

..........................................................

..........................................................

My favourite numbers

..........................................................

..........................................................

..........................................................

..........................................................

Stick your concert in here.

## Me and JBiebz

Stick your show photos in here.

Maybe you've seen another great artist at a concert or festival. Write all the deets in here!

.................................................................................................................................

.................................................................................................................................

.................................................................................................................................

# JUSTIN BIEBER
# WORD WORKOUT

Justin has gone undercover in this jumbled word grid! Study the square closely, then try to find each of the ten words below. The letters could be running in any direction – forwards, backwards, vertically or diagonally.

| U | E | V | E | I | L | E | B | U | D | T | S | V | J | N |
|---|---|---|---|---|---|---|---|---|---|---|---|---|---|---|
| P | A | G | F | Y | A | L | S | V | S | E | H | H | A | E |
| A | Q | E | B | C | B | H | F | A | D | H | B | C | D | V |
| C | D | A | O | N | T | A | R | I | O | W | E | V | B | E |
| N | B | L | F | S | A | W | V | T | S | D | C | R | E | R |
| R | H | G | A | D | G | V | A | W | F | T | F | A | B | S |
| F | A | V | O | R | I | T | E | G | I | R | L | R | V | A |
| D | Z | V | A | M | A | R | I | A | H | C | A | R | E | Y |
| C | T | W | H | W | C | A | F | G | C | V | E | T | W | N |
| A | F | S | L | V | D | M | F | A | X | L | Q | V | B | E |
| N | O | Q | Q | A | C | S | F | B | J | L | I | W | Q | V |
| A | B | I | E | B | E | R | F | E | V | E | R | Z | M | E |
| D | U | P | K | E | A | D | S | N | K | L | R | E | V | R |
| A | S | Q | F | H | A | H | A | R | N | V | C | N | M | U |
| Q | S | E | A | N | K | I | N | G | S | T | O | N | A | V |

ONTARIO
USHER
BIEBER FEVER
NEVER SAY NEVER
FAVORITE GIRL

BABY
SEAN KINGSTON
MARIAH CAREY
CANADA
BELIEVE

"Will you finish it? Never say never!"

# NEVER A CROSS WORD WITH JUSTIN

This tricky crossword will test your Bieber knowledge to the limit! Work through the clues, filling in the grid as you go. If you get stuck, the answers are waiting on page 56.

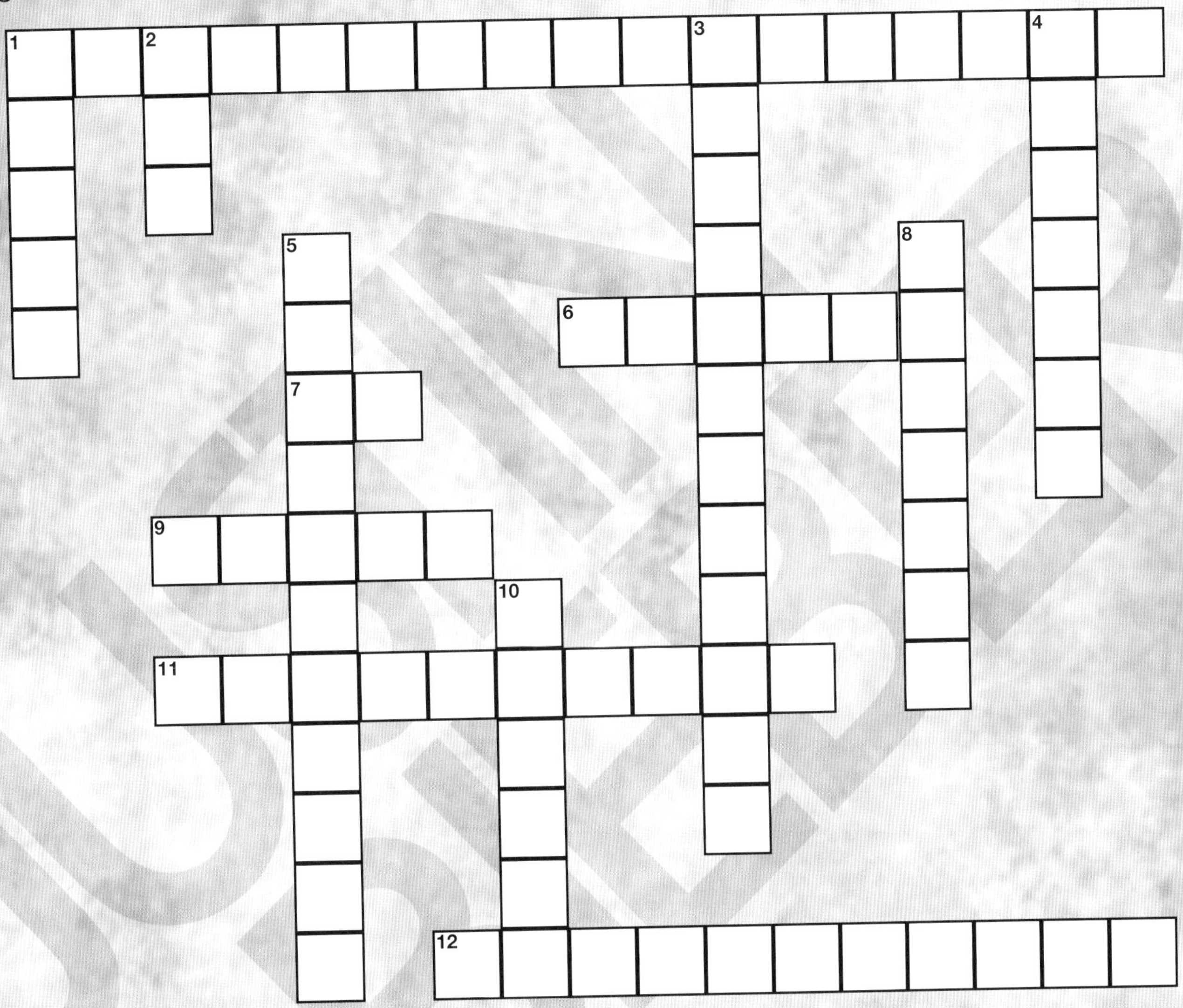

## Across

1. The title of Justin's 2011 Christmas themed album. (5, 3, 9)
6. The name Justin's Mum, Patricia Mallette, is better known as. (6)
7. The song with the shortest title Justin has ever recorded. (2)
9. The last name of JB's girlfriend and the star of Wizards Of Waverley Place. (5)
11. The surname of a reality TV star with her two sisters who made the headlines when she admitted in a tweet that she had caught Bieber fever. (10)
12. Justin and good friend Sean Kingston collaborated on this track for the album 'My World 2.0'. (11)

## Down

1. The name of the R&B star widely thought to have discovered Justin. (5)
2. The record executive who was the first to be hip to Justin's talents once worked for the legendary American record label, So So _ _ _. (3)
3. The name of Justin's long-time manager. (7, 5)
4. The title of Justin's debut single. (3, 4).
5. The song that Justin worked on with Busta Rhymes. (7, 3)
8. The name of Justin's album for 2012 (7)
10. The track that JB recorded for his beloved fans that appeared on his first album. (1, 5)

# And The Winner Is... Justin Bieber!

**It's time to add winning awards to the long list of things that Justin's great at! In just two years he has won an unbelievable 58 major music awards and been nominated for another 65! Not bad going for a young boy from a small Canadian town.**

## American Music Awards, 2010

Justin had an incredible time when he attended the 2010 AMAs with his mentor, Usher. By the end of the evening he'd walked away with an amazing four awards, rocketing himself into the world's attention. Justin was named the "Artist Of The Year", the "Favourite Pop/Rock Male Artist" and the year's "Breakthrough Artist" while his album 'My World 2.0' was named the "Favourite Pop/Rock Album". Wow!

## MTV European Music Awards, 2010

Looking fresh-faced thanks to a new haircut, Justin showed it didn't matter where the award show took place, he could still take home the big prizes! This time he was picking up plaudits at the MTV European Music Awards in Belfast.

## NBA All-Star Celebrity Game, 2011

Justin was thrilled to attend the NBA All-Star Celebrity basket ball game in 2011. As well as getting to rub shoulders with fellow celebs like Rihanna and Lenny Kravitz, he was also named the match's "Most Valuable Player"!

## Teen Choice Awards, 2011

Justin set tongues wagging around the world when he attended the 2011 Teen Choice awards with his girlfriend Selena Gomez. The pair had first appeared in public together the Vanity Fair Oscars party but were so touchy-feely at the Teen Choice Awards Justin nearly missed out on collecting his awards!

## MTV Movie Awards, 2011

The success of Justin's film Never Say Never 3D has meant he has been able to attend some major movie awards shows, too. At the 2011 MTV Movie Movie Awards the star picked up the "Best Jaw Dropping Moment" award from funnymen Danny McBride and Aziz Ansari.

## Billboard Awards, 2011

Justin dominated the 2011 Billboard Awards. He won an incredible six awards on the night and was nominated for four more on one of America's most-prestigious nights for music. Only Justin's own jacket could match his glittering success!

## Brit Awards, 2011

When Justin flew into the UK to attend the 2011 Brit Awards, he earned himself the trophy for "International Breakthrough Act". JB was made to feel at home when fellow Canadian pop star Avril Lavigne climbed up on stage to present him with his award.

## Juno Awards, 2011

Being a proud Canadian, the Juno Awards hold a special place in Justin's heart. The annual awards are the biggest night in the country's pop calendar and Justin loved returning home to catch up with his loyal fans! On the night he picked up the "Pop Album Of The Year" and "Fan Choice" awards.

## CMT Awards, 2011

Don't think Justin is simply a pop artist! In 2011 he also won a major prize at the Country Music Television awards. His reworked version of 'That Should Be Me' with country band Rascall Flatts won the "Collaborative Video Of The Year". Justin took his mum Pattie with him to collect the award. Aah!

# Now The Winner Is...

# Me!

This special page is a place to celebrate your own awards and achievements. Have you won a certificate? Passed a tough test? Got a great report? Don't be shy, if it's something you're proud of, pop it in!

And I'd Like To Thank:

............................................................................................................................

What's the scariest thing about winning an award? Making the acceptance speech! Compose the speech you'd like to say if you were called up on stage.

............................................................................................................................

............................................................................................................................

............................................................................................................................

............................................................................................................................

............................................................................................................................

............................................................................................................................

............................................................................................................................

............................................................................................................................

JUSTIN BIEBER

# SMALL SCREEN STAR

Whilst promoting his music, Justin has been invited to appear on the biggest TV shows around. Here's a tour of JB's top telly!

## Late Night With David Letterman

David Letterman's nightly chat show is a US institution. Everyone who is everyone has been on! Justin's appeared on the show on numerous occasions and has used his quick wit and natural charm to win the viewers over every time!

## The X Factor Live

There are many different versions of the X Factor around the world and Justin has appeared on most of them! Last year, he performed a live duet with a finalist on the American version of the show, then tore the house down on the German version!

## The Today Show

Appearing on so many TV shows isn't all work, work, work! JB had a great time hooking up with Usher on this US daily breakfast show in November 2011. The pair were there to promote their new singles, but they decided having a laugh and joke together would make better viewing

## The Tonight Show with Jay Leno

Letterman's TV rival is fellow comic-turned-chat show host Jay Leno. To prove he isn't taking sides in their battle for ratings, Justin has performed and chatted on Jay's show several times.

### Did you Know?

Justin has also proved his strength as a promising TV actor - taking roles in two CSI: Crime Scene Investigation episodes

# BIG SCREEN IDOL

After you've conquered pop and made yourself a household name on television, where do you go next? The movies, of course! Justin's first film Justin Bieber: Never Say Never 3D was an instant box office sell-out

## It's A Smash!

Any nerves about how the film would be received were quickly laid to rest when the film started holding premieres. Thousands of fans turned out to watch the film and try and catch a glimpse of the movie's star. Here Justin greets clamouring fans in Paris.

## London Calling

Ever since he first burst onto the scene, the Brits have always had a soft spot for Justin. Thousands of Beliebers turned up to show their support at the London premiere of Never Say Never 3D - one of the only documentaries to be a hit at the box office

## Decking The Director!

With the pressures of filming over and the movie about to become a huge global smash, Justin decided to let off some pressure. At the Paris premiere he interrupted an interview his director Jon M Chu to start an impromptu play fight!

# TV Tastes and Film Favourites

Were you one of the fans crunching popcorn and cheering at the screen in 3D glasses at Never Say Never? Use this page to record the shows and movies that you love to watch again and again.

My top five TV shows are

1. ..............................................................................................

2. ..............................................................................................

3. ..............................................................................................

4. ..............................................................................................

5. ..............................................................................................

The best thing on TV ever is ..............................................................

because ..............................................................................................

The one show I can't stand is ...........................................................

The best soap is ..................................................................................

The person in charge of the remote control in our house is .......................

My guilty pleasure (the show you should hate, but secretly L.O.V.E) is

..............................................................................................

My favourite actor is ..........................................................................

My favourite actress is .......................................................................

The best movie in the world is ............................................................

The last time I went to the cinema I saw..............................................

The five films everyone should see are

1. ..............................................................................................

2. ..............................................................................................

3. ..............................................................................................

4. ..............................................................................................

5. ..............................................................................................

# BIEBER LOVE!

During 2011, Justin started being accompanied to red carpet events by a woman other than his mum, Wizards of Waverley Place star Selena Gomez! The couple insist they're just having fun together, but is it more serious than that? Take a look at the pictures and decide.

STAR GUESTS

Although there had been rumours that the pair were seeing each other for some time, Selena first appeared on Justin's arm in public at the annual Vanity Fair Magazine Oscars party.

SMILES UNDER THE SPOTLIGHT

Justin and Selena seemed totally into each other, and completely unaware of the photographers when they attended the MTV Awards together last year.

TOP SECRET

SAY CHEESE!

The couple have been introduced to a variety of Hollywood royalty during their evenings at red carpet events. One highlight has got to be saying 'hi' to Brooklyn, Romeo and Cruz - the gorgeous Beckham boys!

MEET 'N' GREET

Justin's clearly not the only one impressed by Selena! Here are the couple happily hanging out with JB's manager, Scooter Braun at an exclusive Oscars party.

I HEART......

Cut out a picture of your secret love and stick it in here. Don't worry, we won't tell!

I ♥ this person because............................................

................................................................

................................................................

................................................................

................................................................

................................................................

# HAPPY HOLIDAYS

When your day job involves travelling the world and you're the owner of one of the most famous faces there is, getting away from it all can be tricky! When it comes to free time, Justin likes to get creative...

## Holiday On Ice

Skating on a frozen Canadian ice rink dressed in heavy protective clothing wouldn't be many people's idea of a nice getaway. For a sports nut like Justin, spending some time at his local club hitting some pucks is the perfect tonic to his crazy life on the road. An added bonus is that when he puts his helmet on, no one knows who he is!

## The Pride Of Canada

Being Canadian, Justin and his Mum Pattie hold the Stanley Cup – professional ice hockey's top prize – close to their hearts. Its nickname is actually the 'Pride of Canada'. The pair once arranged to take some time off from their busy schedules to visit it in New York.

## Seeing The Sights

During a trip to New York, Justin was able to combine business with pleasure. He was booked to turn on the famous Empire State Building's Christmas lights. While he was doing it, he got the chance to see the city's skyline from a truly unique vantage point!

## Having A Ball!

There's no sitting around with your feet up for Justin Bieber! He prefers to jump in at the deep end and challenge himself. When the star landed in London he arranged a tour of Chelsea Football Club with his friend Reggie Yates. He even had his soccer skills tested by star players Fernando Torres and Frank Lampard.

## On A Roll

While on a tour of the Far East with his mum Pattie, Justin was given some downtime in Taiwan that gave him the chance to indulge in another of his passions. Forget finding a secluded beach or a hotel with a luxurious swimming pool – JB spent his free time skateboarding!

## A Classico

The Chelsea trip whetted Justin's appetite for football, so he was delighted to be asked to spend some time training with the Barcelona team in Spain. As if that wasn't enough of test, he even challenged first team player Bojan Krkic to a game of one-on-one!

# DREAM DESTINATIONS

Do you like to get up and at 'em like the Biebz when you've got time off, or do you prefer to sit back and chillax in the sun?

Fill this page with all of your personal holiday highlights.

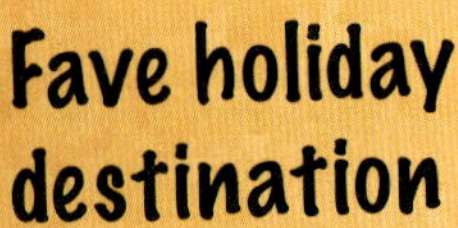

Fave holiday destination

.......................

My travelling party

..................................

..................................

..................................

..................................

..................................

..................................

Stick or draw your holiday pictures here.

## My holiday highlights

..............................

..............................

..............................

..............................

..............................

..............................

Stick or draw your holiday pictures here.

## The thing I love to do when I'm away

....................

....................

....................

## Places to go back to

1. ....................
2. ....................
3. ....................

**The holiday of my dreams would be:**

..............................

# ANSWERS

## Page 22: Lost In Lyrics

1. We're just friends
2. My biggest weakness
3. Stay on the ground
4. I'm on the beat
5. I had a winner
6. Forever
7. Meet you half way
8. Adore you girl
9. One to ninety-two
10. Stay at home by herself

## Page 22: Name that JB Tune!

1. G
2. A
3. D
4. H
5. F
6. B
7. C
8. E

## Page 40: Justin's Word Workout

| | | | | | | | | | | | | | | |
|---|---|---|---|---|---|---|---|---|---|---|---|---|---|---|
| U | E | V | E | I | L | E | B | U | D | T | S | V | J | N |
| P | A | G | F | Y | A | L | S | V | S | E | H | H | A | E |
| A | Q | E | B | C | B | H | F | A | D | H | B | C | D | V |
| C | D | A | O | N | T | A | R | I | O | W | E | V | B | E |
| N | B | L | F | S | A | W | V | T | S | D | C | R | E | R |
| R | H | G | A | D | G | V | A | W | F | T | F | A | B | S |
| F | A | V | O | R | I | T | E | G | I | R | L | R | V | A |
| D | Z | V | A | M | A | R | I | A | H | C | A | R | E | Y |
| C | T | W | H | W | C | A | F | G | C | V | E | T | W | N |
| A | F | S | L | V | D | M | F | A | X | L | Q | V | B | E |
| N | O | Q | Q | A | C | S | F | B | J | L | I | W | Q | V |
| A | B | I | E | B | E | R | F | E | V | E | R | Z | M | E |
| D | U | P | K | E | A | D | S | N | K | L | R | E | V | R |
| A | S | Q | F | H | A | H | A | R | N | V | C | N | M | U |
| Q | S | E | A | N | K | I | N | G | S | T | O | N | A | V |

## Page 41: Never A Cross Word With Justin!